WHEN THE LIGHT
New and Selected Poems

Geraldine Mills

WHEN THE LIGHT
New and Selected Poems

When the Light
New and Selected Poems

is published in 2023 by
ARLEN HOUSE
42 Grange Abbey Road
Baldoyle
Dublin 13
Ireland
Phone: 00 353 86 8360236
arlenhouse@gmail.com
www.arlenhouse.ie

978–1–85132–308–1, *paperback*
978–1–85132–309–8, *limited edition hardback*

Distributed internationally by
SYRACUSE UNIVERSITY PRESS
621 Skytop Road, Suite 110
Syracuse
NY 13244–5290
USA
Phone: 315–443–5534
supress@syr.edu
syracuseuniversitypress.syr.edu

poems © Geraldine Mills, 2023

The moral right of the author has been reserved

Typesetting by Arlen House

cover image:
'Famine in the Land'
from *Parable of the Prodigal Son* 2004
by Hughie O'Donoghue
is reproduced courtesy of the artist
Photography: Anthony Hobbs

Contents

9   *Acknowledgements*

CARRIED

17   Wipeout
18   Form
19   Snowy Owl at Blacksod
20   Stone Whisperer
21   Your Last Days
23   I Keep Looking
24   Some Days (I)
25   Precipitation
26   Invitation to My Sister
27   To the Father of my First Grandchild
28   Hazel
29   Screech Owl
30   Gatherings from the Fadden More Psalter
31   Hawk, Thrush, Worm
32   Some Days (II)
33   When the Light
34   Revenant
35   Leaven
36   Irish Water
37   Moon Struck
38   Side Effect
39   Music
40   Flood
41   Taking Itself Back
42   Some Days (III)
43   Carried

from *Unearthing Your Own* (2001)
47   Portrait of a Woman Weeding
48   Between Women

49 Zeus Thwarted
50 Undertaking
51 In Search of Place
53 A Cappella
54 Ciotóg
55 Something for his Granddaughter
57 Immigrant
58 Grass Breaking
59 Henwife
60 Unearthing Your Own at Céide

from *Toil the Dark Harvest* (2004)
65 Masks
66 Your Poem
67 Iphigenia
68 Naming of Him
70 Intruder
71 Casting Off
73 Stretcher Board
74 Out of Old Stories
75 In a Far-off Mayfly Season
76 The Potter's Field
78 Riverbed
79 Annaghdown Drowning, 1828
81 Flock Memory
82 Astrolabe
84 Fruit Falling
85 The Tree Forgives the Axe

from *An Urgency of Stars* (2010)
89 These are the Only Journeys
90 Changing Ground
91 War of Attrition
92 Any Talk of Eden Must Include the Serpent
93 Sometimes a Woman
94 Invasion
95 Hephaestus

96   A Soft Day in Guernica
97   Fox Woman
99   Word Stitching
101 Reading my Father's Hand
103 A Trick of the Light
104 Flight
105 Mrs Monet Cleans the Lily Pond
106 To Ground
107 Naming the Houses
113 Afterthoughts of Stars
114 Mother and Daughter Triptych
117 Look, We Have Come This Far
118 Where You Meet Yourself
119 Girl on a Blue Bicycle

from *The Other Side of Longing* (2011)
123 The Centre Cannot Hold
124 When the Time Comes
125 To Name It Twice
126 Threshold
127 Side-Fold Dress at the Peabody Museum
128 Summer Solstice
129 Get a Life, Mr Rembrandt!
130 Stanzaberry
131 Conquistadores
132 Common Ground of Ocean
133 Song from an Unnamed Boy

from *Bone Road* (2019)
137 Hunger for Somewhere Else
138 Leaving
139 Outfitted
140 The Ship's Manifest
141 Witness
142 To Each Man
143 To Each Woman
144 Scattering

145 According to *The Globe*
146 Beyond the Whale-Way
147 Word Comes Back to Mr Tuke
148 On Seeing Brown's Cash Grocery
149 Cotton
150 Above their Station
151 In Time He Realises
152 He Longs for Bog Cotton
153 Rain over Achill
154 Reflection
155 Going Back
156 Things to Do When You Go Home
157 Forsaking Tuke's Future
158 By Design
160 Parting Promise
161 The Arch
162 Phthisis
163 Starting Over
164 Belmullet the Talk of Byzantium
165 Home
166 Margaret, 1889
167 Blighted
168 Jigging Up a Storm
169 Let Loose the Fire
170 Butter Stamp
171 Pearl
173 Legacy
174 Waiting for Our Grandchild
175 Bone Road

from *Bone Road in Word and Image* (2020)
179 Hometown

181 *Notes*
184 *About the Author*

Acknowledgements

The author wishes to thank the Arts Council for awarding an Agility Award to complete this collection.

My deepest gratitude to:
Alan Hayes for his constant support.
Hughie O'Donoghue for his perfect cover image.
Peter Moore, James Joyce and Susan Rich for their invaluable feedback on many of the new poems.
Tina Mills-Ledwith for her typing skills.
My heart's best treasures, Peter Moore, Geneviève and Jake, Lia and Lowen, Daniel, Jenny and especially April who has inspired this book.
Máire Bradshaw and Bradshaw Books.

Acknowledgements are due to the editors of the following journals and projects where versions of the new poems were published:
The Irish Times
New Hibernian Review
Washing Windows: Irish Women Write Poetry (Arlen House, 2017)
The Lea-Green Down (Fiery Arrow Press, 2018)
Crannóg
Skylight 47
Shorelines Festival Exhibition, 2021
The Telephone Project
Southernmost Point Guest House
Live Encounters
Crann
Soundings from the Shelves

for April Mary
born to bring light in the dark of winter

When the Light
New and Selected Poems

CARRIED
new poems

WIPEOUT
i.m. Eva Saulitis

The woman
moves away from where she was made,
to Prince William Sound.
Something about it smells of home. She stays.

Each spring
she watches the bay for her orcas,
named after the mountain that welcomes them,
spots them along the shoreline, seal-hunting.

She gets
to know them,
      voice by voice,
      tail by tail.
She is in her element:
            theirs.

Soon
she learns that in this place
of islets and exposed rock,
of weeping forests, cloud-layers,

that
there are more ways to wipe out
a species than to harpoon them:
let the oil tanker sidle in,

let it
bleed the blood of fossils
into the Sound and see,
how in twenty years,

not one orca pup born.

FORM
for Jenny

A leveret slips into our potato patch at dusk,
infant coat the colour of turned earth
where it shapes a bed, cradles into it,
eyes making ready for the night.

Nothing scares it away,
not our switching on of the light
nor our standing to peer out through the glass
at this unlooked-for lockdown visitation.

We fall into sleep, dream our own dreams.
Half-way to being, the moon beams its myths upon us,
as we try to forfend our hearts
from the losses we know will come.

Dawn. Stars with their backs turned
and we go out into our world
of dripping ink caps,
of honey fungus

where the little hare has left us
nothing of itself but
the cold crucible of ridge
in which it had lain: its form.

Snowy Owl at Blacksod
On 14 March 2017, Rescue 116, a Sikorsky helicopter of the Irish Coastguard, crashed into Black Rock off Blacksod, County Mayo, while undertaking a rescue operation. All four crew members died.

The following year finds us near that place
where a farmer hushes us towards a different view,
his clothes the colour of sedge, of moss,
tussocks of red on his cheeks,
as if he had grown from the very bog.

Through his binoculars we finally see it,
perched against its perfect camouflage of rock,
– the snowy owl –
here in the Erris tundra, safe from predators,
other than gawkers like ourselves.

The farmer tells us how his first sighting had been
one white and barred feather, too big for other birds,
and then the bird itself. How he has waited
for its return every springtime since,
when Arctic plains begin to put on their green.

Of the sky tragedy that bleak March night we say nothing.
The unmapped rock, helicopter falling, crew lost.

I zone in on the bird's dark blade of beak, yolk-yellow eye
disturbed by our voices – its warning to lift –
then a great wingspan of white
rises into the day, its satnav mapping the air,
out past the lighthouse, towards Black Rock.

STONE WHISPERER
for Ronan

He reads like he reads his own breath
which stone to choose.

Balanced in his hand, he knows its heft,
lets it become a living thing in his palm,

while lichen hangs clean from hawthorn
and wood anemones brighten at his feet.

Whether he picks the stone
or the stone him, who is to say?

But he listens to each one,
hears when it will meld with the other

and in that way the wall is built.

Your Last Days
i.m. Hedy Gibbons-Lynott

I text you:
morning is so faithful.
It comes back to us
after being away all night.

*

Your acanthus has begun to grow in its pot,
the one you dug up on a good day,
put in a Jiffy bag, posted to me.

*

Yesterday, I waved at the windows
of the hospital,
just in case you were looking out.

*

Last night walking home,
the rain washed all the stars
out of the sky.

*

In the woods, fox-prints
running through the mud.
I heard you were sitting out today.

*

The sky has cleared. There are stars.
I bring you on my walk right now.
You, me, and the night trees.

You text back:
I can see them in my mind's eye.
imagine them waving at us overhead,
their blackness against the last sky.

I Keep Looking
after Patrick Kavanagh

Every young girl I see reminds me
of my daughter when she was
sloughing off her mantle of youth
to step into this world she would master.

The slip of a thing on the Ha'penny Bridge
who smiled at me was one
(when others rushed by, heads bent, no apology)
her nose stud – a newfound sun,

and the little mite only last week,
who waved from the top of the bus
as if to remind me I do exist,
within my house of dust.

Or a day when the stropped blade
of wind sliced up along the quays,
a butterfly tattoo between forefinger and thumb
dropped a coin in my shivering cup.

Every young girl I see
in school uniform or knee-torn jeggings
might one day say to me
'I am still your daughter.'

Some Days (I)

unannounced

    I burrow

    into

    the wild

    animal

of myself.

Precipitation

I carry a mountain of cloud on my shoulders,
patches of fog drizzle along strands of my hair.
I open the window and rain tumbles onto my head,
thunder hangs its coat behind the door.

The weather forecaster speaks like Sylvia Plath,
tongueful of words hailstone-sharp,
clipped as the north wind that fells elms.
My mind has visibility greater than ten miles.

Indigo nimbus, cumulonimbus, violet storms
shatter the bee box under the bed,
wings, limp from damp, swarm
onto the floor, buzzing.

Invitation to My Sister
i.m. Bernadette Padden, d. 22 May 2016

After this night of gales and broken stars,
your silence rises from the dark to sit with me.
All these years, it's time you told me where you went.

> Please come back, tell me all.
> Please come back singing.

Come in your little gold car,
the one that whizzed you through
the curling roads of Erris,
your one good eye seeing you safely to your door.

> Bring your Mayo accent with you.
> Make sure you come back singing.

Wear your pink-loud dress, the one
you bought on Fordham Road
when first New York cajoled you in,
thinking roses, roses all your life,
not briars scratching out your future path.

Come like the fieldfares to our garden in October
with the scent of winter on their wings.
Come with the guelder berries blazing,
the lark still in the clear air
and we'll walk to the place of bees.

> So, why don't you come back now?
> Why don't you come back singing?

TO THE FATHER OF MY FIRST GRANDCHILD
for Jake

Nothing as beautiful as the picture of you
anchored by the weight of your new child
in the harbour of your arms
where she now safely sleeps,
Neptune protecting you both,
her tiny breath rhyming yours.

HAZEL
for Anne, Lillian, John, Tina

Drawn to the wildness beyond our back garden,
we scaled the stone wall of the everyday
into the forbidden world of the other,
scenting on the wind that hazel shells
had already ripened, turned nut-brown.

Feral, hunter-gatherers, we knew nothing of its lore:
how Hermes carried its sacred wand;
made Fionn Mac Cumhaill the clever clogs that he was,
or how poor demented Aengus was off wandering
in the grove where he was bewitched.

The diviner's rod within us doused
the magic of their abundance.
The way a flick of the thumb against the bract
surrendered a perfect mahogany from its sheath.

When we had foraged all that we could,
we settled – like small wood animals –
on the cushions of moss beneath the underwing of tree,
our chosen stone nestled in the bowl of our palms.

The sound of shells cracking
drove the collared dove from its perch
as we eased out each perfect kernel.
And, oh, the taste, the bread of angels,
a midden of hazel husks gathered at our feet.

SCREECH OWL

The owl is sounding out his *O* all night.
Has memorised the sound of your sleeping.

Lets his vowels fall through the open window
where a breeze might enter, if only there was one.

The gecko flitting up and down the shutters
washes her old skin in the shadows.

Tongue-lick of moon hangs in the sky.
Night falls into you.

GATHERINGS FROM THE FADDEN MORE PSALTER
for James and Martha Joyce

And who it was who hid it under there?
Leather strap rent by the digger's maw,
calfskin cover, wraparound, button clasp,
papyrus lining, worlds from where it grew.

How the book fell open on being found
by the metal bucket, then lifted into light.
How the painted eye of eagle must have blinked,
seeing day after a thousand years of night.

Maybe he was not alone – that monk –
perfecting yellow in the eagle's eye,
maybe others shaped the D, the B,
beyond the find place in a midland bog.

Quires of psalms eaten by sour turf,
folios appeared, no more than vellum fronds,
when the iron gall of ink dissolved the skin
yet preserved some letters, almost one whole page
absolved.

As each blessed word began to be released
(from the monk's scriptorium) *Beatus, Deus,*
the fragmented phrase first recognised by all:
in valle lacrimarum – in the valley of tears –

Hawk, Thrush, Worm

Sparrowhawk lies dead on the gravel.
A foot away from her – thrush,
still between its beak the remains of worm
that it pulled from the lawn, unsuspecting.
So full of grub, thrush didn't hear the raptor's wings,
talons ready as she swooped.

Puffed up by her catch, hawk didn't see
our house, the expanse of window,
or maybe the glass mirrored a rival making off
with her prize and so she struck.

In my hands, I study her warm brown breast,
the saffron cere of her beak,
the way she holds her head, quizzical,
eyes wide open, as are those of thrush,
both staring at what is about to happen.
Worm, sightless, sees nothing.

Some Days (II)

unannounced

life comes

          rushing in

to sit at my table.

When the Light

The woman lays down her torn coat.
Its worsted cloth still holds:
marks of blood,
heat of tanks,
stench of shockwaves.

Her hands take the man
pinned to the shadows,
places his coiled grief
along the fabric's length,
(a spring unloosing). Waits.

When the light comes
– and come it does –
she helps the man stand,
walk away from the blood.
Tiny threads of hope take to the air.

Revenant

I had come to the place
where the trucks stop for breath
and the sky was the colour
of earth crash. Burnt.

There were melons piled up on the stall,
small crimson mountains
protecting me from the invasion
of mosquitos waiting to eat my face.

Out of a red pickup I saw
tumbling back, an old man.
What I noticed was his hollowed-out stare.
On his baseball cap, the outline of a deer.

Dandelions had finally turned into clocks
and I pointed this out to the man
who had the jaw,
the nose of my father.

Do I know you? he asked with a voice
I hadn't heard since I was eight
and he had taken his belt to me
for crossing the road on my own.

How was he to know that every time
I have crossed a road since,
I see its escape,
its way to somewhere safe.

LEAVEN

Hungry for the scent of that summer
I bring to the bowl a measure of flour,
white as the deer I startled in the woods
the first day I was allowed
beyond the two-kilometre limit.
Add ferment, wait out the proving.

In the kneading of the dough,
I yield to the starter memories
– Ibiza, San Josep, its baked earth –
the clay oven where you slid the pale rounds
from the wooden paddle onto the waiting coals,
oranges like errant planets falling at my feet.

Afterwards you showed me how to clear
the spent ash from the crust base,
reminding me that each loaf must let
the invisible perform its own alchemy:
to expand, raise, lighten.
If not for this, you said, *no bread could become itself.*

Irish Water

And what about the poor lad sent over on the ferry
to install water meters on Inis Meáin,
only to find the whole of the middle island,
– walls, gardens, fields – made of pure rock,
erratics flung up by the ice age,
landscape criss-crossed in grykes.

He takes the long point of his jack hammer,
certain he can drive it in,
pulsing up and down, up and down, throbbing,
till the sweat breaks out through his *hi-vis*,
droplets drip from his hard hat,
but no soft yield, no soft yield at all
from the frigid clints of the karst.

J.M. Synge above dreaming of playboys,
the farmer with his cow in Dún Fearbhaí,
cormorants in a black huddle on the old pier,
all whisper their constant protest –
*you can't put a measure on an island,
you can't stamp a barcode on the sea.*

Moon Struck

The moment wolf-moon grips the burnished throat of sun,
the cats cower, the birds frenzy their call.
They sense its lunar teeth

before its light (hitting the kitchen)
begins to silver breakfast cups and plates,
before its ice-cold enters our house.

We move in whispers through the rooms, afraid
to look up, even through the pinhole of colander,
for fear wolf-moon will take the eye out of us.

Pulling courage to our shaking hands,
we stand in the night-lit field, hammer the saucepan lids
as the beast moves in for the kill.

The din fills every inch around us, as does the dark,
but we keep on beating and beating
until wolf-moon is on the run.

Then one more strike, one final clang and we watch it
drop the sun from its jaws, slink away,
our world turned, back to day again.

Side Effect

While I sleep,

    the weaverbird

        in my scalp

builds his nest

        from my hair.

Wefting

    and warping,

he plucks out

    strand after

        aching strand.

In the morning

    he has flown,

    the matted nest

abandoned

        on my pillow.

Music
for A.M. Kennedy

Our mother came from a house hopping with it,
all four girls sang, all eight brothers played the fiddle,
brought back as gifts from their father's season
of potato picking in Girvan.

Somewhere along the way,
the flame of it was smoored in her,
but I saw it spark again after a five-dollar note
came from New York for my birthday.

She – who was good at coaxing things –
put me on the back of her bike,
cycled in the Headford Road, through Woodquay,
into the Four Corners, pedalled home again
with an accordion and me on the carrier.

It was winter. She played by ear.
She took a living coal from the kitchen range
and carried it to the grate in the good room
where she inveigled another fire out of it.

Then she started, squeezing the tune from wherever
it lay hidden in the closed case of her heart,
her lips moving silently, as if savouring
a creamy caramel, whose pleasure

she wanted to prolong, tasting
each note before she let it melt down her arms,
spill into her fingers and slide
across the cheap melodeon keys.

After, she held it
like she would a child,
while we reached out our hands
to gather in the warmth.

FLOOD
for Joan Hogan

Rains tumble from clouds they once were,
        explode riverbanks, uproot roads.

Turloughs uprise in fields,
        swallow a whole village.

Swans fly in, make their home
        on the roil of new lake.

A fisherwoman rows by in her boat,
        reels in all the sounds

that float up to her
        from the submerged:

a mother cradling her child,
        the man shaving his chin,

the hymn of the solitary bee,
        the cry of the lost boys.

She rows around day and night
        her world awash with their tears.

She knows no place to rest them, can hear
        their silence pleading:

Let us see the wind,
        please let us smell the stars?

Taking Itself Back
... For too long we have stretched the bowstring of air.
– Miroslav Holub

Give this house a year
and the wild will reclaim it as its own.

Already, bats fornicate inside the cladding,
fly through twilight-spin to midge-fest.

Goats' willow, fluent in the language of survival,
notches seed in a gryke of pathway, sprouts life.

Leafcutter bees have sawn leaf-rounds
from primrose, verbena,

stuffed them into every crevice of the gable end
with the same precision a dentist packs a filling,

sealing in their precious future
while snails bivouac underneath the sills.

Someday, a brace of hunters will battle briars
– like heroes in a Grimm's text –

find walls held up by the tensile strength of web,
swallows in eaves, eggs hatching all over the house.

No trace of the man and woman who
held wildness within themselves

and bargained with nature to keep its distance
as long as they lived there.

Nothing but a sloven of empties on the back step
where squirrels whooped it up on hazelnuts.

Some Days (III)

unannounced

joy

just

bubbles

up

Carried

Someone is saying a prayer for me this day.
Somewhere a palm opens to receive
the bread and offers it up for me.
A jar of honey arrives through the post, intact,
as if delivered by the bees themselves.

> Outside a skying pavane of hope, of feather,
> speedwell sprigging along the thin soil.
> In Kylemore and La Cartuja, the nuns sing
> my name into their psalms,
> candles in Chartres send steadying flames my way.

Someone somewhere makes fennel soup,
sends Hadji Bey's Delight from the English Market,
the holy oil of smile, word, card,
scarlet fringed tulips, orchids,
April teaching me about myself.

> The hare comes every day. Looks
> towards me through the high grass.
> Unafraid,
> before he shape-shifts
> into Mike Healy's field.

Somewhere a woman takes up a crochet hook, thread,
works her own faith into every coloured stitch,
a mantle for my shoulders,
socks of possum fibres,
a necessary hat for my naked head.

> I could not know till this
> how a person can be carried,
> can be borne by the grace of a settling hand,
> a message with the sound of the dawn sea.
> A good belly laugh that could split stitches.

And now this day,
as your constant arms guide
me across our living room floor
to the music of Piazzolla's *Oblivion*,
all these gifts I pass back through my heart:

>recalling when I was wheeled into
>the operating theatre, there was more
>blue sky from the three windows
>than I ever expected. More
>than I ever thought possible.

from
UNEARTHING YOUR OWN
(2001)

Portrait of a Woman Weeding

Spring on a late day in a garden
overcome by scutch, creeping buttercup,
thistle full of head.
With tip of trowel a woman
follows tracery of weed,
cards moss like wool,
unearths earth,
cat on her shoulder sleeping.

In pursuit of the deep tap of root,
she unfolds into the air a scent,
sweet, citric, snapped with longing
from an iota of leaf,
that for one moment becomes
baked-soil sunshine
glinting off white walls.

A man opens shutters
onto a garden scarlet with bloom,
plucks and carries them to her
where she sits eating oranges,
without memory of what it would be,
to touch heavy, waterlogged black of clay,
hear its squelch under boot,
its thud on coffin.

BETWEEN WOMEN
*for Naoko Nangou and her mother**

This is the wedding kimono
I fashioned you.
Flaring dragons, Nippon red,
praying for the day
when you would barter
camera for children;
develop safe domesticity.

I never dreamed
that I would secret it
through war-torn country,
overcome hostile mountains
to the spot
where the Mujahedin
have buried you,
take you from this foreign soil,
dress you,
let the flames marry you
to the Afghan sky.

While I am left
with the leavings of your soul –
your skull, your ribs,
to take you
from this broken land,
back to Tokyo.

* Nangou was a Japanese photographer killed in Afghanistan in 1988

Zeus Thwarted

1

Afraid to look back lest she would see
the white whirr of wing pursuing,
she ran.

Water dripped from her thighs
still stinging from the sound of downstroke,
flattened beak against her throat
before feathers first touched.

To shed the smell of god,
beyond the trees she rolled in the cleave of earth,
bitter cleavers chewed
to rid her of the taste of swan.

2

She holds a picture of a woman bathing,
in a lake that falls and swells with flood,
as she sits with her friend, Leda,
in the safe of afternoon.
Heads bowed they paint their nails,

no vestige of struggle,
no evidence under fingertip
or scent to warn her friend.

Undertaking

These are the difficult days
in this still unnamed house
on the edge of the bluff,
where silence hangs like an osprey
above this table laid out for one

that was once a coffin door
found in every home
(to take the breadth of man
and the last of his breathing)
bought one evening late
in a junk shop in Connecticut,
when you should have been home by six.

Day over night in your work shed
you undertook to strip and sand,
till shavings bled with Indian red
from your plane
while a base carved from bothering bits
turned it horizontal.

Of all your work it was your best,
taking my palm to guide it
along its exposed grain,
ring it round each knotted whorl,
before we sat at it to eat.

In Search of Place

In language not quite said I learned from birth
that we were not of place.
Did not like locals have
the maps that charted lines of lineage
buried around tribal walls.
We spoke in accents not the Galway way,
nor any other needed to mark us in.
Lived in a house where the walls dripped
with the constant sound of lacking.

Our mother lived for letters from New York,
which promised greenbacks to hold a slate wiped clean.
Yet she the very one who cried and said:
they were badly off to write to her
their flight was booked for June.

Wallpaper cracks were patched up once again,
good linen borrowed from one who was of place.
While faces pinned to the front window
watched for the first sound of Ruddy's car
that drove to Shannon to bring them back again.

We rolled in the words they brought with them:
cookie, mall, and faucet. Found faucet
the one I could never translate
no matter how I tried,
for the rain barrel was tapped to nothing but the sky.

I saw New York at eleven when my father died,
a man still out of place,
and aunts who needed to be kind
tried to ease small children lose the chart of him
stretched out, lips blue,
my little sister screaming when she kissed him cold.

Jackie Kennedy and our mother were widows together,
and photographs taken in her black dress
that she wore all that year and never touched again,
showed she looked more at home
on the steps of St Patrick's Cathedral
than cycling the length and breadth of the hazel road
for bread and milk on tick.

I could not wait to flee
holding my breath until the train crossed the Shannon,
and I could sigh again in the soggy foreign air
of Gardiner Street.
Left behind the sharp taste of ripe nut,
wild strawberries foraged from out-of-way places.
To walk streets where being a stranger came easy,
and my heart knew nothing of the way home.

A Cappella
for Tina

When her elder sisters took her to Mass for the first time
and stationed her between them on the hard bench
that prayed for the repose of the soul
of Timothy Leahy and his wife, all she saw
was the hunch of headscarves and the back of the priest
going hell for leather through the *Gloria*, the *Credo*,
deaf to the voices, sweet as angels, that sang
a cappella high in the heavens of the choir.

Back to backs, she faced mouths round with *Hosanna*,
returning each note given divinely
which she gathered in the cupped hands of her heart
until all the air filled in around her with hymn.
Cheeks blazing, her sisters tried to force her
to be content with the craw thump, the genuflecting backs
in front of her, but they could not,
for she was new and full of song.

Ciotóg

We were equal once. Closer than sisters.
From the same egg. Mirror images.

Together then, freedom was the brazen dress we wore,
hitched up around our knees
as we rolled one over the other
down sun-sifted hills.
Took turns to race snails up and down the step,
cradle bird a robin in willow twigs.

But she came, black-beaded, leather-strapped,
proclaimed you chosen,
I unclean and sinister.

Split apart, I watched
as you tried to shape
fat sluggy 'Bs', matchstick 'Ks'
let letters stumble off the page
collide, spill over.
While I stayed trapped behind. Broken. Usurped.

For you were now the right-bright shining one.
I, the hand of the devil.

Ciotóg: Irish for left-handed

Something for his Granddaughter

A 'Jew's Harp', a golden leather money bag, a cobbler's last
were all this man bequeathed who had nothing else to give
but one picture of him taken at the station –
that was miles along the platform
in my tiny child's mind. The green
and cream of my coat collar,
the angora cap around my sister's face
pressed to his rasp of skin in the tiny photo booth.

Little scraps of letters to his angels,
posted from some Paddy place
in London, after the sweat of the building site
was washed away in the cold drip of shower,
bottles under the bed. Sat by his chair
when he came home at Christmas-time,
summer, and watched him clear a plate
of bread fried golden on the crisp of rashers.

There is a twang of 'Jew's Harp' half-remembered,
the silence of his money bag after he had emptied it
in the waiting hands of the nuns.
Promises to take us to Australia
when the dream of work was there; broke
secrets at the gable end to anyone who'd listen.

The cobbler's last is all that's left of him,
rusting among the shed's forgotten tools,
until my daughter's dance shoes demand heel taps
and I dare try what he did when he came home
as father, drew us in line with our shoes,
upended sole by sole, heel to toe,
examined, mended, to hold another six months.

So, it is I who levels now, bright metal shape,
with awl and hammer get to work,
holding the pins at the edge of my mouth,
paring, piercing, tip-tapping
to drive the final nail home.

She slips them on,
hearing the sound in her feet,
riffs, wings and time-steps across the room,
straining to mark the timbre of stage floors
from Lackagh to the edge of her dreams.

Immigrant

When I arrived
the scorched august earth
chilled my skin
as I rasped in the thin air
of my new world condo.

No redemption came
from the masses of sprinklers
that misted the parks.

It remained so while
fall flashed through
the Rouge Valley,
blush and cinnabar
hiding its aridity.

Then white shrouds
unfurled to balming,
while snowploughs
choked the 401 and
letters came all too slowly.

Till one morning in May
and late for work
I stopped to bless
my first green glimpse.

GRASS BREAKING
i.m. Eamonn Padden, d. 28 January 2000

Like frozen grass when trampled snaps and breaks,
yet hangs on hope to see the bright of day,
this body, too, its fragile image makes.

An imprint on the cell is all it takes,
to shatter life spring out in sad array,
like frozen grass when trampled snaps and breaks.

And takes this hurt, all other it forsakes
to pardon pain; a price it dares to pay,
this body, too, its fragile image makes.

When small men give no voice to their mistakes,
the silence in the bones cries with dismay,
like frozen grass when trampled snaps and breaks.

No answer heals the heart that ever aches,
why the blade was splintered who can say?
This body, too, its fragile image makes.

All will stand whole whenever new day wakes.
and questing souls have gladly found their way.
Like frozen grass when trampled snaps and breaks,
this body, too, its fragile image makes.

Henwife

She would make something of herself –
a confidence of lace at her wrists,
sheets that held no memory,
feathers in her hat from hens that filled
her tin canister with coins
when she sold their gifted food,
walked with an air of one going up in the world –
so that he grew bitter and afraid.

She searched out under lonicera, behind loosestrife,
the secret laying places of Rhode Island Red,
Blue Silkie, watched them with an eye canny as the fox
that she skinned with the pearl-hafted knife.

When she caught a fever from scouring the ditches
around the old rath for her best layer
on a devil damp day in March, and took to the bed raving,
he said she had been taken by the fairies;
made this known to neighbours when she spat back at him
the herbs boiled in the new milk of biestings
and would not say her name;

so that when he called her a third time out
of her fever to vouch in the honour of God
that she was his wife, and no answer came,
he hauled her out of her bed to the fire
and swore to all and sundry afterwards
that as the flames pecked the new threads of her chemise
and her screams rose up with the smoke
he had burned the changeling out of her.

with gratitude to Angela Bourke for her gift of The Burning of Bridget Cleary

UNEARTHING YOUR OWN AT CÉIDE*
in memory of your father

You came in search of stone-agers,
farmers who striped
the landscape with their lives,
forest-fellers bolstered by peat
till *sleán* sparked against stone.

You strained to look so deep
you almost missed the shards
so close to the surface;
to be lifted out
by name and cheek bone,
dusted off the memory of a local,

who unearthed for you
fragments of a boy no more than ten,
stitched to the pin-edge of cliff,
stoning seabirds at Céide,
his only way to ease the road
from Glenamoy to Ballycastle.

Drawn by the promise – not
of bog people underfoot, but
of a mother waiting
in a home not hers (nor his),
minding others' children, making lace.
To measure his stretch of three months
since she last called him hers.

Piecing to your past this speck of find
where you and your sisters gathered round
to watch him set a boiling bath
upon chairs, stripped to the waist

and sheets of *Western People* held the heat
while the next kettle boiled.
Fed your belief that the pages
that rose and flapped
were seabirds over Céide.

* Céide: *a Neolithic site in County Mayo, Ireland*

from
TOIL THE DARK HARVEST
(2004)

MASKS

Disturbed by the rain, the woman clears
her table of all domestic things,
turns clay into nose, chin and forehead,
gouges out sockets where the eyes should be.

They look out blind from the earth in her hands
as she listens to the hum of her washing machine,
familiar and safe, taking out the grime
of her home, her children, her working man.

Brown earth faces line the shelves of her dresser,
she lets them dry, jaw to jaw, on the draining board,
in the deep window ledges like scones cooling,
the colour of Mayan gold, on the mantlepiece.

She tears up the floor boards and buries them
with beans, amaranth and cotton.
They stare back at her through the cracks in the timbers
as she steps from stove to table with fresh coffee
or turns to draw the curtains on the night.

Your Poem

Those secret days, those nights –
your body spooned to mine
like wild honey – made me beautiful.

Even in your sleep you rhymed my eyes, my thighs,
my hair that strayed across your face
that I believed I was your queen and you, my falconer.

Here in this stolen bed, the sky tossed with tercel feathers,
you held my face as if it were
your precious bird come home

till your wise mouth tasted salt, and you went back
with stardust in your eyes, for all to see
though never guess, it was I who was your lure.

I was your poem when all the lines were mine,
the lyric of your body mine,
the stanza missing in between. The hidden.

Iphigenia

There is no myth in how the storm squalls round the house
or how the gods are out for blood but
something will change the mind of winds tonight.

They howl like demons at the windows of my room
while the boats wait restless in the bay, and I know
as sure as rain beats off the grass that he will come.

He will stand beside my bed and say there is no other way,
that I have known the way he looks at me
with no father's eye, while I pass the bread to him

so that my mother will not guess,
or if she does, holds nothing
of how he will use my sweet breasts,
my limbs to be lifted high by the elders,
gag my mouth with a cord,
heedless of my cries.

There is no myth in the knife sharp as daffodils
spearing the frozen earth that he will hold to my neck
where a lover might kiss the part of neck
that lovers kiss, my hair pulled back.

He will say it is the thing that fathers do to daughters
so that he can quell the sea, watch his fleet set sail
then put money in an envelope to appease the guilt within.

But how I long to smell the frost rise from the grass
or hold my child that will never be,
(not become a name that dies for Troy)
to watch her pull down apples from a tree.

Naming of Him

My mother is giving away her past. To one of us
a china cup and one her thimbles, to another
again a woven afghan she once had stitched with surety.

She is putting in order before she goes, old letters, receipts,
rent books, references for work when work was in it.
There is nothing here of her London days:
a door closed on sirens, windows sandbagged,
her new years of married life,
or how she took the mail boat with her first sons
to a house safe in the west of Ireland.
She returned just once,
a decade or so after this photo was taken
which she hasn't shown us till now,
one touched by the shadow of winter.

This is my past though I am not in it.
Bundoran nineteen fifty, out of season, but enough work
across the border to keep my parents settled.
They go into Sligo for the day, have tea in a café,
he buys her a coat, she feels beautiful.
They come back, laughing, with a camera,
the only one in the village, take photographs
of the ducks flattening spring cabbage,
locals with bundles of sticks on their backs, their children.

They stand with a backdrop of willow,
my elder sisters and brothers
age two to twelve, all eyes cast down, except Jimmy.
He looks, holding his dog, Pedro,
straight at the lens of the new camera,
as if he can tell beyond this day of promise,
full of sweet cake and apples from Sligo town;
to another year in a Birmingham street,
the car he doesn't hear – its impact.

At eighteen I went in search of him,
London in the seventies,
my first summer job on Half Moon Street.
All I knew was the call that came to the priest's house
while my mother was in town that day
and how he told her, coming out of a shop
laden down with Christmas buying.
The mail boat journey back along to bury him.

I took the tube to Harlesden Station
and found the cemetery from receipts
that came year after year for its upkeep;
then walked line after line of marble names and numbers,
found nothing of where he entered and too quickly left.

INTRUDER

The night the heat drove you to take
your bed onto the balcony,
when the wind came in off the sea
roughing the leaves of the tamarinds,
I didn't follow.

Separate we slept with nothing to soften
the insistence of cars on the street,
and separate I woke to the sound
of the sun coming up over the lagoon.

A sparrow had come in the night
and settled as close as possible,
in the crumble of sheet beside you,
as if she couldn't bear to be without you.

I watched you both –
the pulse in your neck now easy,
your arm nesting her head
tucked into her breast, plump with sleep.

Sensing my breath in the air
she opened her wings and flew from you,
leaving behind some soft imagining of her self
curved and pale.

Casting Off

That November he started leaving it all behind:
bonfires, hideouts, his body streaked with charcoal,
spearing the grass, boy hunter,
or in flippers, snorkel, deep-sea diving,
the unfathomed territory of the kitchen floor,
two Coke bottles tied together – his air tank –
the shark in him swimming away.

To hold him back, I spent the day
collecting firewood, kindling.
He stood by, no coat,
shoulders hunched in the frost shivering
while I worked to try and get it going.
The fire smoked, flamed for a little while.
He went back to the house.

Maybe that's why I brought him hawking
to a school of kestrels, peregrines, tawny eagles,
a Harris hawk called Wexford.
The falconer showed him how to fasten
the bird upon the leather gauntlet,
lace through the rungs in its claws,
then round his own fingers. Tightly.
He learned its need for raw flesh
how it flew from tree to tree
wind hover
without sound
swoop
to whip the morsel from his outstretched fist.

Then my turn, the gauntlet on my hand,
the bird upon it, me nothing more than a branch.
We walked through the woods, my arm raised,

elbow by my side till we came to a clearing
mellow with beech leaves.
The bird, its golden beak, its autumn wings, waited.
I stretched out my hand
and moving it up and out, cast off.

STRETCHER BOARD
for Ness

The chance of it happening again –
you and me meeting on the street like that
both rushing to different ends,
you drinking coffee as you went.

Your shopping list could have been
your martingale, holding your head down
as you hurried for green paint and butter
and tablets for the horse.

You had fifteen minutes
which we filled with talk of Vettriano,
how he never got to art college either
and look at how well he got on.

We checked out old postcards in the antique shop:
Andalucía nineteen-o-five, washerwomen
wringing their dirty linen in the sun. Loggers
from Vancouver lumbering pine into carts –

till memory gripped us by the cuff,
your sons and mine trekking across the mountain,
never to be so beautifully young again,
the sun a halo round their hair, and shining

on the remnant of canoe above your kitchen door
frog and sea creatures (Indian red) carved in high relief,
that your grandfather brought back from the Haida.
A stretcher board you said, made to keep two sides apart.

OUT OF OLD STORIES
The Shadow and the Heart

These days the skies hurt with blue,
the flames of earth are lifted and carried
across the stone terraces that reminded you
of fields around Leam, Recess, Gortacarnaun.
We have never known such heat, the locals say,
*and look how the snails sit tightly packed
as corncobs on the top of fence posts.*

The mulberries have injured us with their juice
like the last time we picked them together;
it bled the length of our arms, down legs,
mixed with the sweat of our bellies.

When out of nowhere, but somewhere, the rain came,
we trapped it in the waiting bowls of our hands
and you told me that if a shower of rain came
while the sun shone, a fox's wedding was taking place.

Touching my face, you turned me to where you said
you saw them coming through the olive trees,
the vixen's flaring tail covered in Queen Anne's lace,
her cheeks rouged with mulberry,
a canny look in the groom's eye

and you slipped away, followed the bridal party
out along the lemon trees, through the chicken run,
strewing them with caper flowers.
Out along the camino, a wilderness of dust
slipped with them down the mountainside,
your basket of fruit spilling onto the ground.

In a Far-off Mayfly Season

Diggers hulk upon our road on their way
to pile drive another foundation into bog.
Our house shudders and all pictures tilt.

Persimmons fall out of bowls,
wine flows back into jugs, a dog into a gramophone.
Footballs caught in triumph slip out of grasp;
the sleeping maid whose pots and pans slide
into the next room beyond the frame
sink below the rising water table.

In a far-off mayfly season a fisherman
will catch his hook in our window frame
and reel in the cleaned bones of it;
he will place it in his boat beside two trout
his box of bait, not knowing

how a man and a woman,
their two children look out at trees
that crouch like a lioness,
a fox blazing against snow,
or where they lay their heads at night,
she in the curve of his sleep,
he closer to the door to protect her.

The Potter's Field

*Too bloodied to be returned to the temple, the high priests
took the silver, the price of him on whom a price was set
and as a burial place for strangers bought the potter's field.*

Thirty pieces were as good to him as a year's work
of cracked amphorae and terracotta bowls
as he looked out over the valley of Hinnom.

Little more than scrub, nothing grew from its red clay
and the one living tree the goats had stripped
of its glaucous, notched leaves.

With the money burning in his pocket
and graves mapped out for strangers
the potter closed his shop, took to making statues.

From the scorched clay of the valley
he smoothed and shaped limb by limb
until the body of a woman formed.
When he went to carve her eyes
they filled so full of heartbreak

his hands shook. At night when he turned to his wife
they haunted him and he climbed from his bed
to shape them into something more of promise,

but they burned with the memory of the angel, a shimmer
of gold on his stockings, gems on his shoes,
the quiet settling of his gilded wings
as he stood his ground by her chair.

The potter toiled, to change them to a day full
of future, not of neighbours walking
the three steps of compassion with her,

men holding their hats over their breastbones
while her son passed with his cross and looked out
over the Hebron before giving up,
the robber free on a technicality.

He shivered as the sky of her eye darkened
and in that time cities, forests, bombs fell,
mothers' milk polluted.

His wife could not bear to watch him dawn after dawn,
his face raw from lack of sleep, turn in his bed, get up again,
all the wine in the world not helping to forget.

He started to ramble up into the mountains,
look down upon the field he had betrayed.
The world turned to clay in his mouth.

Riverbed

There was an arm's length of bed between them
and no way of telling how that came to be,
or why this August day when he awoke
his hand reached out to touch the familiar
of her skin and rising, they drove
across blankets of bog, a cluster of arable
till they came to a river with a rock
that jutted like a peninsula
into its centre just beyond the bridge.

Within the shelter of its bank
of bog and *dobey* stuff and shale,
they laid their sleeping bags on the flat bed of rock,
smoothed by its element to pillow their heads
and the yield of their bodies.
He covered her eyes from the glare of the sun
and they slept to the deep river voice,
warm and remembering, like some singer
from a radio piece long ago, turned down low,

while the noon sun arched over them
and a hiker sat on the bridge with his lunch
before he tackled Máimeán,
gave them up to their sleep, the water
folding and unfolding around them
like bolts of silk, silver with purple thistle heads.

Annaghdown Drowning, 1828

... Ach lá chomh breá leis gan gaoth ná báisteach,
lán a bháid acu 'scuab ar shiúl ...

Antoine Raftaire

My scarf would have saved us that day,
tamped in the wound of wood ribs
where the sheep's foot foundered;
would have held the lake in its pheasant's eye
if not pulled out; that man's coat stamped in place
with such force, the ribs let out their cry, cracked.
In the frame of sound I saw my basket
with fresh eggs, butter newly-salted, sink.
The pheasant's eye that only ever knew the hair
of my head floated off, its jade neck darkened.

I let go of the scarf that kept my head warm
when the winds blew in the gap of the house.
I was a hand waving to the last of sky
above the Corrib, Menlo, Bushy Park.
I let go of a sky that showed me kingfishers;
the echo of gulls on their way to the sea.
Let go of the small grasp of my son holding
as the dog licked cracked eggs off my boots.
I let go of the tips of my fingers, the last of me
to breathe air on that September day. Touch
the world on my skin, hairs on my knuckles standing.

Sheep sank (bubbles of bleating from their mouths)
and like white rocks from some foreign beach
filled the hole waiting in the deep for us.
The man who gave his great coat to the gash
so close to the shore, longed for its return,
to cover the skin of his back gone cold;
but the sleeves ballooned, fish swam through
their coral reef in the western island lake,

emerged, were shape of those who drowned before us.
We sank into them, scarfskin turned silver,
from scale into gill. Changed, became fin skin.

Flock Memory

He lost the way of working with his days;
no white stones of sheep to count at night,
no anxious dawn to pull a sickly lamp,
the prize ram culled, the raddle on its back
wiped out when Herod's lackeys came.

A new flock wouldn't know to move from field to field,
track the scent of grass through the gap in the wall
nor find the stone fort on the hill to shelter from bad days,
where Ann Farrell and her baby lay.

In spring the hawthorn won't draw them close,
as magpies sit and watch white petals fall
like bones into a flame; a notice on his gate,
a snag of wool on wire.

Astrolabe

This was the way Hypatia taught me:
to cut and shape the flat disc first,
calibrate its scale around the edge,
get its arm to pivot and by degrees
I'd learn the time of day.

Each life's hour I worked on it
blind to darkness emptying outside,
attached two eyeholes matching up the sights
till day came spilling in.
I brought it to her, my gift,
and what she saw as competence was love.

Though she argued that beauty was illusion,
all of Alexandria talked of hers,
the men with longing, the women with their scorn
as they gathered in the marketplace
to count the scales of fish or sniff out spices
as good women do.

They watched to see her white cloak pass
and mock us young men running to her word

and mocked us still when forced to find
the eye within; but the I within me
could only see the sky blue of her own,
the curve of breast beneath her cloak.

To unlearn this weakness in me, make me rise
above the flesh, she rubbed my nose
in her soiled and bloodied underclothes,
but the instrument of my body
calibrated to my want
just made me want her more

till whispers started seeping from church walls,
her name from mouth to ear like wasp stings.

In darkness when souls turned black
and days of fasting were posted on the door,
I came out to focus on some unknown star
and setting up my sights
saw the man with a black shell to his ear
whistle to someone on the lower balcony
as her chariot came down the street

and know it was too late to cry *Hypatia, Hypatia,*
my voice lost while Christians oozed from shadows,
pulled her from her carriage, their oyster shells
like razors to hack her flesh to pieces.

Nights, I stand in the marketplace
watch the sky above me inscribe her chariot,
her cloak white across the firmament,
I take out my astrolabe and with its sharpened arm,
pluck out the eye buried deep within me.

I would have the sky lash me with its stars,
the world spin off its axis
never know the time of day.

Fruit Falling

It is the morning of my daughter's leaving.
She is still asleep,
her cases in the hall eager to be gone
while I have packed all I will
into the seed purse of her memory.

She leaves stars on the floor for me to sweep up,
sky fires fallen from some show,
some moment when she shone.

Haws ripen, guelder swells with the future,
apples shiver in the waiting light,
are learning the language of letting go.
She will find her own fruit, pick and eat it,
follow its scent on the wind.
I am a small branch bending.

The Tree Forgives the Axe

We wouldn't fail to leaf in this place,
cut willow staked in the ground
puts out green in the new season.

When crossed by wind
we lean like old men into one another,
when things are good we grow.

We hold in our heartwood our strength to stand,
witness in our ring of life the way
the world was then and now;

how Solomon showed his wisdom,
when Gandhi walked to salt.
Jesus healed. Martin Luther had a dream.

We make good the air from jets
that streak the sky,
while women in blue burkas
hurry home before curfew.

We watch clouds collude,
let our leaves fall like bodies
from towering oaks.

When chopped and nailed into a cross,
we still forgive the axe.

from
AN URGENCY OF STARS
(2010)

These are the Only Journeys

That winter had one month too many.
Each day brought storms that plundered,
the window panes iced over,
the cold came too close.

It was the season when our children left
to slip into their own skins.
If they stayed, they died.
There are no other journeys.

With no shelter to hide behind,
there was cold enough for both of us.
Like seals, all we could do was
breathe holes in the ice to survive.

Changing Ground

I have spoken to no one for days
but the small bird with the black band
of neck as it bobs its way in front of me;
it feigns nesting in the torc of wrack on the sand.

A man in a scrapie wool jumper
picks broken teeth from the strand;
if he opens the black cavern of his mouth
and utters three, two, even one word,
I'll be gone with him.

The day comes when you can no longer
squeeze into the old coat of yourself.

Slievemore stays where it is,
never moved its whole old life.
It waits for the farmers to shift
their animals up and down with the seasons.

My bones know change the way birds know sky,
the way they let go of light over the deserted village,
the way the grass knows it, bitten down to the quick.

WAR OF ATTRITION

Left with one more axe to grind,
and no whetstone,
she went to his room and the small glass
where his teeth were sleeping.

She used them now and filed real slow
until the axe, honed and stropped,
was all steel gleam,
the teeth a millimetre short.

Returning them to their rightful place,
she walked out the gate,
the taste of a wet summer in the apples,
and he all talk, but no bite.

Any Talk of Eden Must Include the Serpent

Everything so Martha's Vineyard,
so clapboard and white cedar shingle,
seen from the *Island Queen* that takes us
through morning fog to the first sighting
of the island's signs that forbid
motorboats their speed,

and Oak Bluffs with the oldest carousel,
all fairground horses and barker's jingle,
houses so wholly pink,
so sherbet lime and lemon sunshine,
beaming down on seasoned stores,
garden seats in the shape of butterflies,
fritillaries for the rich that, with a bit of luck,
we might meet the Clintons on Music Street.

Talk of the monied and famous
includes those with their own osprey nests
– Pulitzers, Carly and Sweet Baby James –
hidden away from our yellow tour bus,
long stretches of shimmering green,
beaches to make films on, but

I saw a woman in the hardware store with a black eye,
though the door she walked into was gone,
and in Edgartown where the shingle
is stripped and painted each year
to keep it the white whaling town it always was,
I could stretch out my hand and touch Chappaquiddick.

SOMETIMES A WOMAN
after Rilke

Sometimes a woman
stands up from the dinner table
and walks out the half-open door.

She keeps on going, though
she doesn't know where,
and the road catches darkness

long before it falls.
Black thoughts she stills
with an urgency of stars.

INVASION

The cicadas' first impulse,
when the ground warmed up,
was to unbury themselves.
After seventeen years, they moulted,

exploded into air. The fierce sound
of their mating pierced the everyday,
with weddings, Bar Mitzvahs,
Cape Cod barbecues cancelled.

Shielded by their coats, people
scuttled from homes and offices,
scared to get caught in the crossfire,
some afraid to venture out at all.

For three weeks they blocked out
the wing sound of buzzard,
loons sleeking across the canal,
the choke of cars on Sagamore Bridge

while all along Cotuit, Clay Pond, Great Neck Road,
the females plundered the trees.
Their cutting jaws made slits in the bark
deep enough to favour future troops.

Foliage turning desert-brown,
the orange strip of their wings
on the small dark tank of their bodies,
as they took the town of Mashpee

where every flag fluttered at half-mast
for its warrior sons, toddlers the last time
these local invaders hatched out. Fiery eyes
now watched them come home in body bags.

HEPHAESTUS
for Daniel

The sun was small fire compared to my smithy,
so I dropped the bellows and went outside
to see its last rays emblazon the olive trees,
the sheaf binders with their armfuls of corn,
before it sank beyond Mount Olympus.
In the weight of shadows along the path
a figure made her way towards me.
It was Thetis, mother of Achilles,
who pleaded with me for her son on the eve of battle.
Born with my own mother's rejection still alight,
a lame god has few choices, so I brazed
for the hero all his mother asked.

Hidden away in my forge,
hammer on anvil, bellows on spark,
I beat from the small volcanoes of my ire:
a crested helmet fit for a hero's head,
a cuirass brighter than the blazing coals themselves,
and a pair of the finest greaves with ankle straps.
I cast a shield five layers thick, and, glazed with sweat,
chased on it earth, sky, a gibbous moon, two cities –
one with a wedding banquet in full bloom,
the other with a herd of straight-horned cattle
savaged by lions who cornered the bull,
tore him apart, lapped up his blood and guts.

When I had finished, I laid them before Thetis
who swooped on them in the way
a falcon grabs an unsuspecting bird.
Now, here is the myth: a mother thinks
she can protect her son. She will read his future
from the corner of her eye, try to call out to him,
but he must tear her armour from his chest
without a safeguard, walk into the flame.

A Soft Day in Guernica

There is something about the way
the townspeople walk through the streets,
umbrellas up against the silent mist,

while we, our heads exposed, dodge spikes,
know nothing of sky or how things can
rain down from it without warning.

Fox Woman

Night and the covert of duvet about me,
a skitter of shadow crosses the room.
With the stench of wet fur and viscera
she brings rain and her shivering body
into the space beside me, tells me

that to save herself she has been running
from those who feared the russet of her pelt,
who went gunning for her as she made her way
back to her cubs in their waiting,
a Light Sussex between her jaws.

The entrance to them earth-stopped,
the baying of dogs on the wind.
She hightailed it across stone walls,
brushed field and sink of bog
to arrive at streets that she slinked through.

The pelt of rain upon pavements.
She pulled coat tails around her face,
down alleyways where huddles
of rags and skats clawed at her
as she scavenged in the stink of bins.

She kept moving, making shadow of herself
by apartment hoardings, through housing estates,
up escarpments to open fields,
back to a cathedral of trees,
this open window.

She cries for the young ones gone from her,
guilt tears for leaving them alone.
I soothe her flaming fur until her mind pictures
their little snouts resting in dewclaws,
as if they had just entered sleep.

Maybe it was their time to go, I whisper
as she curves herself to my back.
Maybe it is your time to live.
My mouth fills with the aftertaste of blood,
between us the reek of vixen.

Word Stitching

Still with the memory of matinee coats
that her mother knit, she started small:

    cast on three fish words
    purled a line of pure water
    slipped a blue autumn

and she had knit herself a haiku.

A villanelle was next
in the softest chenille

    although she worried how to shape such rhyme
    read every pattern in her mother's book,
    ripped and unripped each minute of her time

until she had shaped the perfect piece.

And there was so much demand
for her sestina that she had to open a shop,
a tiny room on the edge of the square
where the chevrons on the pavement
matched the patterns that she wove,
repeating the same word stitches.

Now her whole world was caught up in stitches,
and to keep with the growing demand
she bought the building next to the shop
that reached out onto the square,
so customers could drink tea on the pavement
while they waited for lines that she wove.

A man came in once looking for a tanka top.
She thought the style was long out of fashion
but he said he would pay her good money for it, so

she stayed up one holy night
to add the extra two lines.

She did a roaring trade in metaphors:
scarves stitched with blackbirds on spring mornings,
their saffron beaks blinding,
crossover cardigans of women soothing
silkworms from thunder.
Gloves with coy murmurings
and grand *randonnées*.

'The Love Song of J. Alfred Prufrock'
caused her such disquiet,
with the women all coming and going,
that she cried when she came
to the purple patch at the end.

   She spun Rilke into silk.

With Billy Collins she had to change needles,
longer, slightly sharper to weave in the irony,

but with Frost she didn't know which road to take,
since there was one promise too many to keep,
so she went for something like a homecoming
in a Wendell Berry stitch
and that made all the difference.

Reading My Father's Hand

So much imagined, forgotten or never even known
comes down to me in these,
each one opening in the same formal way,
I hope this letter finds you well, as its departure leaves me,
learned no doubt on those rare days
when he chose school over *poitín* time in the bog,
his hair black as the hops in the still,
strong hands even then that went
to haul bricks onto lorries in Oxford Street.
Trudging home through the smog to a silent room
where he laid down words on the plumb lines
of blue Basildon Bond like rows of McAlpine blocks.

Penned to them all the promise of what he earned,
saved, wired each week to the west of Ireland;
decrying the days when he couldn't work
for the weather, or the pain, and how
the ganger sent him back to his digs
that gave him no light, no lock on the door,
and the rain coming in through the roof
for thirty-five shillings a week.

I follow his shadow down the scaffold of each page,
where he names what it felt to be held up against
the wall with a knife blade of loneliness at his throat,
and fight back with nothing
but the brown neck of a bottle;
hear his voice in the cadence of Mayo accent
that even on paper carries a surfeit of syllable
in the word *childeren* that he had too many of

and the promise of that registered envelope so clear
that to touch scrim now reminds me of the way it held
its grip on ten pounds until collected in the post office
on a Wednesday in ordinary time.

As God on the cross flew out of the sky
carrying His own blood from the smell of lonely places,
I read the loss in the hand
that ended each note with a crosshatching of kisses
no schoolmaster would ever allow.

A Trick of the Light

Splicing together cine footage
from the sixties onto DVD,
my cousin presents me with my past.
This film holds everything:
breath of my mother, stretch of my sisters,
my brother young and at home.

The black of Mrs McGaugh's shawl
that hides her face from the lens,
milk churns in the back of the cart
where she sat me and wrapped me on days
when the walk from school was too long.

The squeal of a gate after Bomber Fahy
dumped bonhams to rot
on that part of road where the tinkers
curved sticks for their camp.
When they dismantled it all to move on,
how I longed to be gone with them.

We standing around at Spiddal mart
with farmers spitting on palms
in the flicker and splice of the screen,
while cows watched me dig into sand
at the edge of the sea, so clear I can taste salt.

The frame of me smiling and something
of mischief in my eyes must be a trick of the light,
for I remember little that is kind from that time,
but a dark box of days, the barrel iced over,
a pinhole of bright in the night.

FLIGHT

His tread
on the stairs that small morning,
the rise of each foot,
the tock of the clock hid his going
out the door she heard close

of the home she spent her whole life
making, the one that couldn't contain
this son she struggled to hold,
who was never at home to himself.

How she searched for some sign of him
in the last of his words she upended,
any thread of him snagged on a bush,
nosy neighbours caught no shadow of him
on a road stitched with pockets of night.

In the dark that she entered,
she prayed to the ones who came back
for a glimpse of him somewhere,
– on a scaffold maybe in Ipswich,
cadging fistfuls of porter in Harlesden,

even finishing a staircase in Mayfair,
his golden head burnished with shavings
after he measured the tread,
sanded the last line of nosing,
the rise of each going,
                    the flight.

Mrs Monet Cleans the Lily Pond

She trawls her net across the green rash of weed,
he watching her from the window in such a frenzy
he will not lift a brush, a palette knife until she's done,
her dress flounced into her pantaloons,
a hat protecting her from the mad Giverny sun.

In the gather of slime, she sees picnics *plein air*
with Mrs Renoir, Mrs Pissarro, though they don't see
eye to eye on dress fabrics or ducks' livers;
Mrs Cezanne, a bit too dry for her taste,
though she has a soft reasoning at the dinner table
when tempers rise, a glass knocked over
spills its red stain upon the white damask.
Then a voice gravels from beyond.

Her net fills with the smell of rotting.
She dredges newts out of their philanderings,
a silt of caddis world, of wandering snail,
a leech puckers to the cold skin of her calf,
while all he sees are blooms full and pert as divas.

To Ground
for Chris Montague

Thinking in verb: to plant, root, settle,
she moved to the place she married into,
five miles from her home, a granite coastline.
Spite in the wind that forced the few trees sideways,
little shelter from the things she tried to shelter from:
rigid jaw, hard mouth, a rock silence
when she hoped to chip an inch of talk
from one of them.

Nights after the house had fallen quiet
she followed the course of her longing
back to that limestone softness;
the way it yielded to the rain
that let its own self dissolve into fields and rivers
rendering leaves of alder and hazel round.

It put nature on horses, built her people's bones,
as if they had drunk the very stone
from which they themselves had grown,
and their faces – always their faces – soft, giving.

Naming the Houses

I

This is what we do to retrieve half-lost, half-
forsaken pieces of ourselves, we go back
into places that are not looked for
until heard in stories that for so long
were just placenames that slipped off
our mother's tongue, as we took apart
the old range out on the grass,
black-leaded it piece by piece.
We believed that every town in Mayo
began with the letter B:
Ballycroy Bangor Bunnahowen Belmullet
Barnatra Bohola Ballina
Blacksod Bellacorick Ballycastle Belderrig,
invoked for us again after a night of disconsolate rain
when a bog was riven from its hold.

It raged down the mountain side, its cold lava
boiling over houses, bridges, silage bales,
a wilderness of *puiteach** over Pollathomas.
Down over walls, a child's blue tractor
swept half the graveyard clean away,
our grandmother's dust washed out to sea
as if her clay self knew to make room for one of us.

---

* *puiteach*: boggy ground, mud

II

In a cold season we five sisters,
carrying the raw death of a sixth,
fulfilled her wish to return to the place of her birth
and find the different houses where our family lived.
To see again the foam in the river which she thought
was from washerwomen upstream
scrubbing their dirty *giobals* on washboards,
soapsuds borne away in the curve of water,
bubbles arriving at her feet,
just as she believed the white droppings on the trees
were from some giant in the sky, who rinsed his mouth,
then spat it out after he washed his teeth.

We took the road from Galway
up through Tuam, Foxford, Ballina,
followed a sky relieved of cranes,
a dearth of white site notices flapping on gates
well before the turn for Glenamoy,
through bogland haunted by the ghosts of old trees
while the copper sedge, a monstrance of holy fire,
burned into the world of our past.

III

Seeds of rain dripped off sheep wire fences
and planted themselves in the sodden earth
beyond the door we looked out of. Feathers
of smoke rose from the one visible house in the valley.
Ruins of others, like rotted teeth, led us to the first
home our mother made, after she had closed the door
on an insistence of sandbags, sirens, curfew,
and in her high heels and London coat
took the boat back to her birthplace
to keep her then small family safe.
Our father sold up all they had and followed after.
They stayed a while in this rain house
given to them by a man from Boola
who had his own way of making potato pits,
small ones by the day, not big ones like the locals did.

Still the shadow of drills in the plot by the door
these walls mapped out in lichens,
witches' butter unctuous on trees
where our first two brothers played,
the black eyes of windows they looked out,
one of them long dead the other gone never to return.
Here for a time our mother used her canny ways
to stop winter dripping down picture frames,
pulled an unkindness of ravens from the chimney
before moving on, lorries loaded
in the middle of the night
to his new job somewhere across the border,
until the next one sent them packing,
back again to whatever house was offered.

IV

Here was our father's first place of belonging,
in the shelter of trees, the home of his cousins.
All we could see: an old suitcase, its lid thrown open,
the shadow of bottles in corners,
the shadow of fire in soot,
the shadow of a small boy sharing a cousin's clothes,
his father dead, his mother living beyond Céide,
paid to talk other boys to sleep in beds above a shop.

We followed the road that drew him as a child
with his brother beyond the cliffs,
the broken nose of the headland to that shop
in Ballycastle where she served and waited for them,
in a home that wasn't hers, children not hers.
Instead, we met the man she reared,
now grown to good old age in his own place.

This quiet man remembered how she was there
when he woke in the morning,
when he came running to her from school,
and there when his parents went to Lourdes in 1923,
gone for weeks, they were pilgrims across countries
searching out the mother of sorrow
– she was already serving shop and other lives,
dreaming of her own sons and when,
if ever, she might see them.

V

Sometimes so little needed to travel back
down through avenues of gorse and rhododendron,
past a river that bore no foam,
no leaves un-spattered white,
roads that knew no traffic to find the husk of a house
where our eldest sister was born.
Just three walls left of this place called the forge.
Her recall of horses coming from all around,
the ferric smell and singe of iron on hoof.
These things in the earth, we heard, half-heard
as we drove down side roads, turned along the cliffs,
to see waves break off the coast of this land.

A man in Belderrig checking lobster pots,
hooked names together like a net,
in no time got the breed of us, our seed,
each generation that carried music in the veins,
fiddlers in pubs, concertina players
making songs of what had gone before:
my great grandmother who came back
from the States after the famine
to this land that had nothing but its own hunger.
She never again travelled beyond Belmullet on fair day,
where she went to sell milk, eggs and apples.
That money bought her a stretch of cloth
for a dress finer than anything ever seen in Holyoke.

VI

Sitting in the church that Sunday
we saw in the high cheekbone, the contour of jaw,
a tracery of connection to the people around us.
Proved we were from the same clay
as the ones our mother talked about
– the lost ones in the cemetery at Pollathomas
that the mountain had shifted that night –
remnants of its treachery still in walls silted up,
holes that showed where it brought
all it could with it into the sea.

We scoured the ground for names, found
Shevlin, Mullarkey, McDonald, Ginty ...
nothing of our grandmother's
but a fragment from another sister's memory
of the fire tongs pushed into the ground
by the far wall to mark the spot where she lay.

We searched all along its length trying to find
what linked us to that part of us gone.
No whit of identity, nothing at all to mark her leaving,
never to know if she were washed out to sea.
So I name her now,
Catherine Deane, our grandmother,
a woman with never a home to call her own,
her two boys separated from her,
one of them our father
who, as a child, walked to see her
with bog cotton to soften the inside of his shoes.

Afterthoughts of Stars

Once while playing in the turned-over barrel
it rolled away with us still in it,
holes in its rusted shell let spectra through
and we fell headlong down the hill.

As we tumbled head over head over rear
we became travellers hurtling into space
holding onto nothing but dust motes
that streamed into our battered capsule.

Out into the orbit of silence
into wispy filaments beyond time,
light years away from knowing
how stars came into being

or that when it came down to it
what were we but an afterthought of stars
clattering back to earth
at the bottom bar of a Ballindooley gate.

Mother and Daughter Triptych

I

Reflection

Whatever way the light this evening bends,
when I look in the window of the train
I see my mother looking back at me.
Yesterday every time the phone rang
I expected it was her telling me
she was already six years dead.

Old enough to be my grandmother,
we never did the mother-daughter thing,
no clothes swopping, secrets, best friends
– mothers are never best friends –
though we shared the same mote
we cast from each other's eye.

Nothing much said but I left as soon
as the brazen orange sins of the spindle tree
confessed themselves all along the path.
I often think the part of herself she feared most
was the part she saw in me.

Now I see how life falls from us in the end.
I measure the life that she weathered,
see her in my neck's shrivel and scrawn,
how I might call for her in the end.
I know if I turn from the window
I will be myself again. I keep.

II

This Life Cut Short

She was never more than a name to us,
our sister's life that was only
the same length outside as within,
a head too big for birthing, tore our mother apart.

Too small for all we wanted to contain,
we ran through trees to gather hazelnuts and berries
or haws when all else failed
to feed ourselves like wildish things.

The whistle of a blade of grass between our lips
went skimming across the bog,
made our mouths tingle,
though gave us breath enough for whispers.

Years later my mother spoke of it
when she came to visit me at last,
my own daughter, sitting *zazen*
on the floor between us.

She cried for a child of hers
who could not make it on her own.
In a world where we fight to survive, she said
a girl has to be able to hold her own head up.

III

Instar

Before your daughter gets to the stage
where she is the nothing between egg and bird,
take her to the edge of the mountain,
light a fire, daub her skin with charcoal,
feed her bitter berries, the milk of dandelion.
Teach her the lore of the fox,
the wisdom of weather. Wish for her:
a spare button for her jacket,
loose change in her purse,
the taste of moon on her tongue,
a lake to mirror her eyes,
St Jude when things seem hopeless,
St Anthony when she is lost,
St Cecilia when she needs to sing,
to keep from missing
the sure heart rhythm of the womb.

Look, We Have Come This Far
for Peter

There was little we packed for this journey:
a fox's promise, the blue of a heron's egg,
bed ends from a skip on Northbrook Road
so full of woodworm we had to throw them back.

Me riding backwards on the motorbike
as we went up through the Sally Gap,
the curve of the Dublin mountains
holding its place on my lap.

Winters when pipes burst and snow lay
indolent on path and rooftops,
we sat before a fierce fire, weaving baskets
while cane suppled in the basin beside us.

You asleep on the last seat of the bus,
I wishing you would wake
so that you could see it too –
the sun burning up the fog at Delphi.

We didn't pack for the children
we gave each other,
one with the language of your bones,
the other with the thin of my skin.

My journey west with them, waiting for you
to someday follow on. When you did,
you had nothing but the shape of my horizon
on which to lay your head.

Look, how we've come the other side of children.
Today as if there were no tomorrows left to us,
you calm me in the way clapped cymbals soothe
the swarming bees. Closer than breathing, we hold.

Where You Meet Yourself

There are days you can't remember who you are.
You spend hours looking for old pieces of yourself

behind the cushions of the sofa, the bathroom mirror,
the eye of the potato, that safe soft place

where you hid the purse of possibility,
but words slip away,

you empty out pockets full
of useless rhyme and incident.

You open your mouth and feathers fall out,
– primaries and coverts into the air.

Lifted up on the thermal of your breath,
they roost in the crown of your head

then take themselves out the window
and play puck with the plums in the high garden.

You try to follow them and meet yourself
coming back with a poem

that wants to give itself to you,
but your hands shake too much to grab onto it.

GIRL ON A BLUE BICYCLE
for Geneviève

Whatever way it plays with dust particles
and scatters out its own wavelength,
this different sky, so blue it is pure self.

The young girl must have taken
a ladder to it and drawn down
the colour the Greeks had no name for

into her eyes, her wraparound skirt,
her bike, as she pedals by me,
the sun falling into her blonde hair.

I follow her down Calle Cielo, up Calle Luna,
the storks lording it over the town
above the lapis dome of the *iglesia*.

Arms that tied me to myself begin
to move out and up like a dancer.
My body, unfolding to the music of heat,

becomes different in this light
as it stretches up to hear someone
sing from an open window.

I gather in my waiting hands the given notes
while the girl on the blue bicycle is so far ahead
of me now she has become the eye of heaven.

from
THE OTHER SIDE OF LONGING
(2011)

The Centre Cannot Hold

All night the wind has fought with our cottage.
It wakes and unnerves a part of me
that is unsettled by such noise,
as it is by all the colours of grey
we must live with throughout these summer days.

But your country has weather big enough for both of us.
It tumbles an outermost house into the sea
to careen on a foreign beach in Chatham,
or a tornado whips up Dorothy into another state.
Hurricanes with names benign as dimpled grand-aunts
come to tea and scones,
but leave you stranded in their wake,
flood you with their grief.

A man once told me about the wind in Oklahoma.
It flung their screen door into Sam Weller's garden,
whipped one blade of straw from the barn
and drilled it right through the glass
of their kitchen window.
It held there, needle straight, the pane intact,
lights blown, food in the icebox melting.

Before its contents folded onto the floor
they were allowed eat all at once;
pistachio, dark chocolate, black cherry,
while the straw lodged tight in its place,
breaking their mother's back.

Our lives are built on vagaries of weather,
one well-aimed gust and the sandbars
of memory crumble at our feet.

When The Time Comes

What of the mountain ablaze beyond our window?
Gorse, burning up the dark, so loud
we fear its crackle, hear its heat.

It spits out seeds that defy flame,
smuts of furze get washed into the stream's source
that tumbles down, picking up along the way:

whirligigs, caddis fly larvae, turf scent,
the luteus light of lesser celandine,
foxglove – that does the heart good just to look at.

It foams by the boundary of our land, so small,
yet there is nothing to stop it from thinking big –
from becoming ocean when the time comes.

Rushing under the bridge to a neighbour's field,
down through bog tannin, it carries into the lake
before it takes itself to the river that flows

around the oarsmen, past the teahouse at Menlo
under the Salmon Weir Bridge,
by the cathedral that still reels in the faithful.

It catches sight of the sea, boats by the Spanish Arch.
Lets go of its name, heads out into the Atlantic, reaches
your coast with the memory of mountain, gorse, fire.

To Name It Twice

My hotel room comes with free drinks,
fruit, the baggage of its number – 911 –
and me looking out at skyscrapers,
a plane snailblazing the blue.

Down below is *iPod Touch* city –
life that can trip on the slip of a fingertip.
Traffic here is so slow it would never
catch on as a video game.

There's breakfast at Roxy's Deli
with towers of waffles, syrup.
Trick or Treat couples
are dancing at Suzy Woos.

Not the way I first saw this city; this city
in the sixties with my sisters and mother
at the top of the Empire State –
the tallest building even then

as we squeezed into the swelter
of the recording booth
to sing damp and cold
out of ourselves; *Galway Bay*

dropping onto the black vinyl 78
that circled round and round.
It gathered each note into itself,
before it played us back,

our voices dancing across the rooftops,
over East River, Brooklyn, the Bronx;
above the skyline of Manhattan
where the blue held no fear of rain, no terror.

THRESHOLD

Not having learned each other off by heart,
we tried to hammer out our differences
into the joists and floorboards
of our half-built house,
into the solid beams across our line of vision

when we lay in bed at night
to watch the dark fall through the space between,
the wind cursing in the cold hallway
ready to wake the kitchen with no hearth,
no spark among the clouds of ashes.

A threshold reached, I left through no door,
two chimneys punching holes in the sky,
black eyes of no windows looked after me
as I walked down no path
past the rows of potato drills
in our good neighbour's field.

The wind coming round the corner
slapped me in the face.
It didn't slow my step,
or the ropes of bindweed
choking the stones
all the way to the beach

where my footprints sank into sand
among the spindle toes of oystercatchers,
while gulls cried above the graveyard on the cliff,
mingling with god, with limpet shells.

Side-Fold Dress at The Peabody Museum

As if it were once mine, lost
and now found after years of searching.
As if I remember the woman tanning the skin first,
whether of elk or caribou I cannot recall.

Then stitching it with rows of porcupine quills
having won the sacred right to dye each piece,
moisten them in her mouth, flatten them,
burrow holes in the hide with an awl, thread them in.

Adding glass beads from Europe, brass buttons,
cowrie shells across the shoulder and little bunches
of red cloth sewn into it, dyed with madder,
all the way from somewhere near these shores,

used in the petticoats of women
from Conamara, Inis Mór, Boffin,
or as *swanskin* – that square of red flannel my mother
placed to my father's back when he couldn't work

from the pain meted out on building sites,
when life was a challenge of rattlesnake
around a bunch of arrows.

Summer Solstice

This is the contract between light and dark,
day and night.
Each accepts when the world belongs
to the other.
This is day's time, we know no sleep.
Swallows, cutting
the sky, are giddy with it.

Touched by the hand of Midas, everything
turns to gold:
common cat's-ear, bird's-foot trefoil,
buttercup.
The sun's monstrance gilds the high garden,
the cherry tree.
A prayer big enough to cover our best selves.

GET A LIFE, MR REMBRANDT!
Artist self-portrait at the Wadsworth Atheneum

Unwrinkle the brow, plump up the lips

Botox the furrow between the mournful eyes

airbrush the weak chin from your father's side
that swarthy nose from your mam's

get the toilet-brush hair gelled

flaunt diamond studs on the left lobe

a tattoo on the rippling biceps
I luv u Hendrickje Stoffels

put the grizzly bear coat up on eBay

ditch the hat
but don't let go of the hands

STANZABERRY
for Lisa C. Taylor and Russ Taylor

You bribed the leaves to hang on until I came
so I could read them in the way they shape you,
otherwise you would have to climb each tree,
stitch them back up there,
match each leaflet and lobe to its own.

But they clung on for me to see butter melt,
claret spill onto branches just above my head,
persimmon leaves outrival their own brilliance
all along the Fenton river, the Grist Mill,
Horse Barn Hill, where I heard Canada geese
spearhead their going in a startle of blue.

Here I learned the argument of squirrel
that tight-roped its way across the limb of tree,
malachite lichen on the house side of trunk,
autumn rushing ahead of me on the road, while

each morning in the warm nest of my room
I woke to the new world
carrying dawn to my window
in a rose glow, blush, uplift of light
– a shrub you had no name for –
but I have crossed an ocean to see it,
so I call it giftberry, carnaberry, stanzaberry.

Conquistadores

Docked on the table's oilcloth
like a ship at some foreign port,
the American parcel landed
to whoops of delight.

Our mother unhitched each cotton knot,
unfurled the sails of strong brown paper,
tore back the cardboard flaps,
letting all hands dive in, plunder.

Banners of lollipops and sweets,
Betty Crocker Muffin Mix
plaid pants, rainbow ribbons,
things we never dreamed of –

eyelash curlers, nail buffers,
'he-highls', 'standy-out slips'
so beautiful they made us believe
we could be someone else.

Dressed up in what we now became,
she frog-marched us across the floor,
our eyes full of stars,
our faces spangled with sugar,

the new world scent
conquering the kitchen,
more exotic than jasmine,
than spikenard.

Common Ground of Ocean

These things we have in common:
the year that we were born,
one son, one daughter, the love of a good man,
listening to Leonard Cohen when we were young
and listening to him still. The fish eye of blueberries,
the sacrament of words.

Each day we go to our chosen rooms
with themes from shared stories
picked up on our morning walks,
where the sea brands poems into rocks
and rabbits breed among the Lady's Bedstraw.

At lunch we eat like pilgrims from Lough Derg
or some such place where we deny ourselves
until the white page has done its holy work.
Pull our chairs to the foot of the fire
and warm ourselves more with conversation
than any heat the turf can give us back.

You tell me of men who spin yarn into afghans.
I answer with yarns that are spun out of *piseogs*,
let our unholy ghosts rise out of the smoke.
What would we call them if only we could name
the ones who have stolen our childhoods?

SONG FROM AN UNNAMED BOY
Letterfrack Graveyard, 2009

When I was a child I ate fire for breakfast,
the dark was a lantern-shaped star
I pulled on a string with the moon bright behind me
through the world with its windows ajar.

The clouds held onto the rain every morning,
the cows looked out to the edge of the sea,
until men told my father I only spelled trouble.
School was the place where my soul could run free.

That lie was a snake, in the wall it was waiting.
When I rattled the loose stones its venom fell out.
Bread that they baked held the sting of a scorpion
eating their hypocrisy dressed up as devout.

My sorrow unmasked, they stamped on my laughter.
I was the lamb being dragged to the slaughter.

from
BONE ROAD
(2019)

Hunger for Somewhere Else

They're glad to see the back
of all the wind-crippled whins,
turn their heads from
the rain over Achill Head,
smoor the final fire.

They've had their bellyful
of stinking haulms,
grateful now to hand back
their hungry piece of grass to the landlord

and watch the dog on a scatter of stone,
a fetch in the tumbled-down *scailp*,
a fling of dunlins on sand
waiting for the boat to sail.

* *Scailp*: earth hut or shelter under rock

Leaving

The longest day still entering their dawn,
they follow the carts of hopefuls
along the famished track
down to the sea.

Beyond the calm waters of Elly Bay,
the *SS Waldensian* lies anchored,
brighter than any golden hoard
offered to Manannán, the sea god.

There are scant tears,
for their passage is paid,
new clothes on their backs,
landing money promised.

The whole family going:
my great-grandparents, six children,
ten-year-old Brigid, my grandmother
– that's Tuke's deal.

Outfitted

Waiting for high water,
the chosen clusters
are ferried by the blue jackets
on the *Seahorse* gunboat.

They leave the bay

then out through
the Narrows of Achill
where the water runs
with unrelenting force.

They climb aboard the steamer,
men in forward, women aft.

Outfitted with a straw bed,
a pillow to lay their heads,
enough marine soap
to wash the whole of Erris
out of them.

A swell builds mid-Atlantic.
Through spume and spindrift, they sail,
fog too thick for soupers,
they sight an iceberg.

The Ship's Manifest

Philip Heveron
Mary Heveron
Mary Heveron
David Heveron
Brigid Heveron
Margaret Heveron
Martin Heveron
James Heveron

WITNESS
'How patiently they bear their want'

When he got home to England,
he wrote to the papers.
Mr Tuke, merchant banker, Quaker,
told them how he had watched

a wraith sitting at a loom
with neither woof nor warp,
shunting the empty frame
forward, back

in a place where the poor sucked stones
from the road, ate their children's hair,
were blown like chaff
into the lake's unsated mouth.

And more failed years to follow,
rain that washed the turf back into the bog.
The best of them with nothing
but a mouthful of meal.

Clutches of begging letters sent to him
hidden under the wings of a hen,
and seeing what he saw
the only hope of their saving

was in the form of a fund
that sent the Allan Line
up and down the coast,
netting shoal after desperate shoal.

To Each Man

one suit of clothes
and to put inside that suit a shirt
and over that suit a coat
a handkerchief to stand proud
from its breast pocket
socks to soften his strong boots
a cap to keep the wind from his ears
a muffler to scarf him from the breeze
as he stands on deck
longing for the ocean to start

To Each Woman

a dress
and to set off that dress a jacket
a shawl to keep her shoulders warm
a bonnet to grace her hair
two sets of unmentionables
soft against her skin
stockings and a pair of boots
fine needles and thread
to bind her to the future

with her dirty *giobals* cast off
now she is all style
the new world will stand
in the snow to look at her

* *giobals*: old clothes, rags

Scattering

some were sent to Fall River some were sent to Poughkeepsie some were sent to Passaic some were sent to Lost Creek some were sent to Wabasha some were sent to Minooka some were sent to Durango some were sent to Painsville some were sent to White Water some were sent to St Louis some were sent to Still Water some were sent to Dunlap some were sent to Winona some were sent to Pent Water some were sent to Woonsocket and North Water Street

According to *The Globe*

Into Boston Harbour
on the Fourth of July,
flags cheering, firecracker boys,
speeches, brass bands,
my people come.
Eyes out on sticks with the welcome
they think is for them alone.

Their ticket says Water Street, Warren,
not far from the great sachem's spring.
The scent of trees, a house with stairs,
the likes they've never seen.

They start over in this town.
Within a week, steady work in the mill,
soon flesh on riddled bones,
shoes for the boys,
white bows in the girls' hair.

If the Dintys back in Doolough
could only see them now.

Beyond the Whale-Way

They step onto sidewalks
a word as alien as the thin sliver of sky
above their heads.
Water from a faucet not the dark mystery of well.

Newness moves around the street
on its own two feet,
willing to let go of elsewhere,
forget the other that they have left behind.

Word Comes Back to Mr Tuke

Good families the letter says.
In fine fettle, happy with their lot,
even the children working in the mill.

Heverons and Monaghans
sharing on the corner
of Water and Bowen.

A stairway in their tenement
makes sure they are going
up in the world.

On Seeing Brown's Cash Grocery
for Diane Heveran Rothaar

First he must roll the word around in his mouth
to taste its hugeness as he stands and peers in the door
of John H. Brown's Mammoth Cash Grocery.

From here the new world bustles out its scent in greeting.
No part of him believes that dreams can be this real:
velvet skin of strange fruits, pelts of stranger animals.
Nine good cigars for twenty-five cents. Cinnamon.

With some of his landing cash still loyal to his pocket,
he sees how he might spend it on tea, on flour, salt or grain
but who in their right mind would spend it on blocks of
ice, or on *cipins*, when there are more trees here
than ten lifetimes ever saw back home.

And what about the earpiece, mouthpiece
clamped to the wall behind the counter?
If only there was its twin in Glencastle Post Office,
he would gladly hand over the last of his Tuke dollar,
crank up the Greek name for 'far' and 'sound'

and wait for that moment
when he would hear across the whale-road
the familiar cadence of home,
tell them that the worst meal here
was still better than the best one back there,
this new life sweeter
than the barrel of molasses he is standing by.

* *cipins:* kindling

COTTON

First the seed
the cream of flowers
pod becomes boll
dries, splits open,
curves back
to expose fibres.

Then the carding
        the drawn slivers
the ginning
        the roving
the sizing
        the spinning
the warping
        the slashing
the weaving
        the spooling.

Sheeting
shirting
sateen
twill
bolts of them
flowing
like rivers
into
Narragansett Bay.

Above their Station

November, and they watch as winter flurries in.
A tracery of leaf, of fern, of crystal cave
etched across the frozen windowpane.

Mary heats her well-earned quarter in the candle flame,
lets the fire from the coin brand a perfect lens
on the frosted glass. A telescope
opening undiscovered worlds into the room.

She sees herself in a landau,
with its Moroccan leather and broadlace.
David, all swanky doodle dandy,
swanning up and down the thoroughfare.

And Brigid (my grandmother),
silk in her dress, silk in her hat,
shading her too thin skin from snow and sun.

They lift little Martin up, and peering out
he can see no carriage wheels, no fancy silver cane,
just chimney stacks balling their fists at the sky.
His uproar has their father rushing in

who flays them with his ire
for filling the child with lies;
his biting words chill their magic screen,
his rimed breath freezes their waking dream,
turns it icy white.

In Time He Realises

they have forsaken
one hunger for another,

mill work ten hours a day
six days a week, all year round,

thousands of spindles
hundreds of looms

waiting to snare a sleeve, an arm,
a tress of hair, lint choking lungs,

the tiniest stirrup of the ear
splintered by such noise.

He Longs for Bog Cotton

That lover of wet places;
some years there was so much of it,
its fruit transformed *puiteach*
into snow-covered tundra.

A counterpane of white above the bog,
picked to soften the inside of his shoes
when he walked to Belmullet on fair days,
flick of hare's-tail all along the sedge.

Rain Over Achill

This night that is all moon –
its light playing puck with him
as he works his way home along Water Street
– spawns a silver river, a glister of fish.

His legs still think they are treadled
to the crank and shuttle of the loom,
the ache in his arms worse than
footing the whole of Doolough's turf.

For one startling moment, he doesn't see
the shingles of each single roof ahead.
Only the cap over Achill Head
when there was rain on it.

Reflection

All this lunar night
the moon's cold seeps into
the emptied glass on the table
on the table itself
on his coat's shoulder
with a dander of lint
the row of small shoes
waiting by the door

where he sees

waiting by the door
the row of small shoes
with a dander of lint
on his coat's shoulder
on the table itself
the emptied glass on the table
the moon's cold seeps into
all this lunar night

Going Back

Does it matter
whether it was the voice
that he heard that night
calling him out of the half-light,

or the black bird on the steeple
(of the church just built)
singing its golden heart into the dawn
as he trudged his way to the mills,

but he bought a passage on a ship
still marked with famine
back to where the swan children
spent their last days,
where the barnacle geese
found their second home.

Things To Do When You Go Home

Untumble the walls of the house.
Uprise its lintel from the overgrowth,
like a calf-skin psalter lifted from the bog.
Unlatch the door.

Unsmoor the fire.
Updraught the embers waiting there
all the while you were beyond the whale-way.
Untether its glow.

Unsour the fields.
Uproot the dock, the poison ragwort, scutch.
Ease the clay back in beneath your nails.
Unhang the rust-gnawed gate.

Unsay the words you felt you had to say
– upsticks – the leaving and the coming back.
Ring the rhyme of scythe along the day.
Unbreak the heart.

Forsaking Tuke's Future

There is a place beyond the dark
where the heart goes when it is drawn
further into a winter it is already in.

Not even two years gone and another child born,
they docked in Cobh, the workhouse,
forsaking Tuke's future.

Land, however blighted, was preferable
to all those factory stacks,
the clank and clatter of looms.

Streets just paved with streets, not the gold
of corn at saving time,
the saffron tint of whin,
mizzle over Erris that he thirsted for.

By Design

How beautiful your drawings, how fine!
Indeed, masterful and ... for that price!
Pray tell me, Mr Wilkinson,
how you come to bear such
a skilled hand for one so young?

> My father, sir, a builder in Whitney,
> learned it all from him.
> My first one standing in my hometown,
> the next in Chipping North.
> Eight of them up and running
> by my twenty-second year.

How interesting, but at the outset let me tell you this,
I want no gaud, no frippery.
We are, as you know, ratepayers ourselves.
These Irish beggars cannot be choosers.
Let them eat scenery if they want pleasing.

> I get your point, Commissioner,
> and have planned for that. See here:
> un-plastered walls, local stone-rubble,
> each quoin and architrave hammer-dressed.
> Floors of mortar and earth more suited to our guests
> since it's what their bare feet are at home with, after all.

Well, Mr Wilkinson – George, if I may –
you have thought of everything. But ventilation!
Perfect calculations of fresh air per pauper!
Is that not stretching it a bit too far?
How can we control the numbers if fever
isn't let race through these structured flues
like wonder flows through summer?

But Commissioner, sir ...

Above all else they must know their place.
Here there must be no lazy beds, no idle hands.

> I have accounted for that just here –
> the yard for breaking stones, for splitting oakum;
> the yard for female idiots, the one for men,
> and here in the comfort of this room they will swear
> that they own neither kine nor cat, scrap nor scraw.

Such luxury, George,
you have planned for them a palace
the likes of which they've never known.
How in all that's good and holy
will we ever coax them to leave us?

Parting Promise
10 November 1884

He leaves them at the poorhouse gate,
their details entered by an exacting hand,
the bad condition they have landed in
ledgered in neat lines and columns.
His is the only name missing
– Philip Heveron, my great-grandfather.

Imagine that April parting promise
as something of him follows
the spoor of his yearning
back to the margin land he comes from,
where rain illuminates every broken field,
every lichened wall.

The dream holds him to the house
he will build near Shraigh National School,
his hands still able to read the shape of stone
and know the place
where he will build the hearth,
feel the weight of his heart against the one
where he will site their front door,
opening away from the wind to shelter them.

The Arch

Through the hard-hip, well-rounded breast of the arch,
their bodies listing, they went.

The women ordered to turn left,
the boys right.

The weight of that ship on their backs,
the cold backwash of its eyes,

the way the streets of Warren
seeped out of their tight mouths,

sea streeled out from their hair.
Bones holding bones.

What could he have heard that night
that brought them back to this?

PHTHISIS
i.m. Margaret Heveron; died in Cork Workhouse, 1885

The word no longer used, the one she died of,
all the waves the ship had sailed across
had entered her before they'd docked in Cobh.

Ocean-flooded lungs, a bloodied cough,
with famished limbs, a fevered brow, they tossed
around the word no longer used, the one she died of.

In the women's yard, her mother could not move
the wall that kept her from her child, a cross
that nailed her since they'd docked in Cobh.

Outside the sickroom window, cold and rough,
they broke stones, the indigents, the dross
who feared to use the word, the one she died of.

A burning bush consumed her, as if God above
had sent Moses to her with its fire, its force
that flamed within her when they docked in Cobh.

To see another day the one thing that she'd love.
The cooling air upon her skin, gone all because
a word no longer used, the one she'd surely die of.

In a mass grave somewhere, no name to prove,
no way to mark her life, repair that loss.
The word no longer used, the one she died of,
remembered here, the day they docked in Cobh.

STARTING OVER

Which road they took
        to find their way back
is lost with them
        but they followed it
till they reached
        their thin bits of living
that they scrawb'd from
        the wind-whipped hollow land.
Erris in their marrow,
        the Mullet in their bones,
as crucial to them
        as breathing.

Belmullet the Talk of Byzantium

This margin land –
no road in or out of it
until eighteen twenty-four –
was once known only from the sea.

On the orders of emperors
and guided by ancient maps,
seamen steered their boats
through the Bosphorus Strait,
the Aegean, battled the Atlantic roil
until they spied Broadhaven Stags,
their landmark and their goal
– the common whelk –

found only on this coast,
not common then
for when 'milked' its sluggish hue
turned imperial in the Erris air,
purple, so vibrant, it put to shame
the heather, loosestrife, vetch.

Worth its silver weight,
the prized last sliver on the spectrum of light,
this empyrean tint was brought back,
brought down to earth
in the swish and trim of regal silks,
and while its colour trended,
made Belmullet
the talk of all Byzantium.

HOME

Morning doesn't break here,
not like over there where it split open
like an egg at the side of a bowl
and out spilled its glair, its brash yolky sun.

Here it breathes its best self into the light,
glints open the first blackbird's eye to sing,
shines through the kitchen window
to the slow hum of waking.

Slips the whole of the sky into its mouth,
holds onto it for all the hours
the new world beyond the ocean
is still in darkness, waiting.

Margaret, 1889

Another girl born
another child
given the dead's name

BLIGHTED

Your name came to you seaward
upon a ship returning home from Warren
where your family never settled.

Against the tide they travelled back
kept hidden in your mother's shawl that sick sister
until the poorhouse buried her.

When it was time to christen you
her ghost name was put to use again,
each of its letters blighted one by one.

You carried her weight on your back,
the flooded ocean of her eyes,
the way the stones of the workhouse
scraped against your crooked teeth.

You heard the cry of her along the lazy beds
as you barrowed swill to the pigs,
caught her on the slant of salt air,
your body listing.

Jigging Up a Storm

They took the boat – the spent clayspade of land
unable to feed those who came after –

back and forth to Scotland to pick potatoes.
Babies born on the winter stretch of migration.

My grandmother met a Henry from Roy
who found work with a seed merchant in Glasgow;

a ganger like others, he returned
each season to recruit the Erris pickers

and when the boat docked at Pickle Point,
unloaded onto the pier chests of tea,

flour, bone china for his wife,
dresses for his four daughters,

fiddles for the eight boys, rosined
and ready to snatch a slow air

from the wind through bog cotton,
or jigging up a storm

that raised the rafters with
each perfect beat, out the open roof,

all the way down to the strand,
all the way over the waves.

Let Loose the Fire
for the Henrys

Hearts ripe for freedom, my uncles, mere boys,
boycotted school, never to return
when the Master called the Irish *savages*.

Choosing instead the three Rs:
rebel, rising, republic

learned from men whom they joined
at the day's dimming
or cycled by with a tip of their cap,

the blacksmith who forged their pikes,
taught them to make dummy rifles,
hid bullets in the frames of their bikes.

The GPO – as far from them as America –
they waited out the days for orders to filter down,
learned the art of taking cover;

then they could shake out
the spark from the ashes,
let loose the fire when their time came.

Butter Stamp
for my grandmother, Brigid Heveron

Tuned to the turn of sound,
to the song of the churn,
my grandmother drew the dash
up and down the cream,
listening for the flecks of gild to form.

And then the butter came.

Washed and washed again, salted,
she slapped it into shape,
marked it with her stamp, the only solid thing
passed down from her to me.

Its grip burnished to sheen from all that use,
my hand folds over the honeyed wood
where once her palm pressed it
into the golden round

leaving a perfect imprint of chevrons,
a cluster of strawberry leaves, its seeded fruit,
and, in that way, overlaid
all that had gone before:
blight blossom, down-lying, poorhouse.

PEARL
i.m. of my mother

The grit that found
its way in under her nail
turned the finger septic

as a young girl sent over
on the boat with her brothers
to toil the dark harvest,

pickers bent over like question marks,
knuckles skinned,
trawling the ridges for tubers

only fit for sleep
after bowls of what
she'd picked, boiled,

sleeping on straw in the women's bothy
to dream of gloves
with jewel buttons, necklaces.

What happened after that
is gone with her except the nail abscessed,
the bed of it infected;

no oyster way to mantle it layer over layer
of nacre, reverse its taint to lustre, pearl.
Instead, lanced and lanced again

it lost its memory to grow straight
but ridged and beaked like abalone
grew a further eighty years

among the perfect others of her right hand,
and funny how laying her out,
the undertaker painted it
mother-of-pearl, lustrous, reflecting light.

LEGACY
for Geneviève and Daniel

My grandmother has come down
through me to you,
lives on in that same jut of your jaw,
that same full purse of lower lip.

Lives on in the family lore
that stops the snowblaze of whitethorn
before it reaches the Maytime threshold,
no new shoes on the kitchen table,
no vexing the fairies with dirty dishwater
nor knocking one small stone from their fort.

So, if I cross your sticky eye
with my gold of ring
or stem your bleeding knee
with ribwort chewed to poultice,
it is because it is the way it was shown to me,
as to my mother,
     her mother
         and her mother
before that.

Waiting for Our Grandchild

We are relearning lullabies,
take our old voices out of storage,
dusting off *angel, night-night, hush.*

The first scan of you on the fridge
is held there by magnets, as you are
to the pull of your father's heart,

your mother's – who comes back to visit us,
gravid with you. Sleeps in the old bed for the last time
where she was first whispered,

safe then within my heart, as you now within hers,
your fingers already formed, your lungs stronger,
your ear attuned to her voice.

She knows it is time to let go
of all her childhood things,
takes the faded posters from the wall

of moments when she shone:
Carousel, My Fair Lady, Miss Saigon,
ready for this new stage of mothering,

while your father dreams
in the too-long days of deployed duty
about when he gets back home,

of driving you both across
the wheat fields of North Dakota
golden as the hair on his two darlings' heads.

Bone Road

If my great-grandparents had not made
that journey back,
some other mother would have been born,
some other me. But they did

and now the pattern repeats itself,
not sea but air, not hunger but heart
that calls our daughter to up sticks,
follow the same whale-way.

This is no fairy story
I will tell our grandchildren
as they wave their spangled banners,
carry lineage in their eyes

of a man, a woman, their six children,
who, grateful for the passage paid,
left behind the bone road, took the boat,
grasped the hand of refuge

waiting for them on the other shore;
and that in-between time
saw their leave-taking
as the only way to find home.

from
BONE ROAD IN WORD AND IMAGE
(2020)

HOMETOWN
for Maggie O'Brien

And what of the family who stayed
in the mill house on Water and Bowen,
the rooms they no longer shared?

                                        They stayed,
eased into the loss of nine absent voices,
let other light find the lack of footfall on the stairs,
the dog of loneliness muzzled.

                                        They stayed,
gave up each year's earnings to the grocer,
to keep as many mouths again fed,
shadows behind, faces to the sun.

                                        They stayed,
stood on their corner street and watched
all three mills go up in flames. Looms to cinders,
spindles to ash, jobs to dust.

                                        They stayed,
pulled themselves up from the hardscrabble,
births, marriages in St Mary's Church, it too rebuilt
from fire. Warren their home now.

                                                They thrived.

Notes

Page 17: Eva Saulitis was a marine biologist and poet from Alaska who studied orca whales on Prince William Sound. She was involved in impact studies as a result of the 1989 Exxon Valdez oil spill. She died on 16 January 2016.

Page 23: 'I keep Looking' was inspired by 'Memory of My Father' and was first published in *The Lea-Green Down* (Fiery Arrow Press, 2018), edited by Eileen Casey, where poets were invited to respond to the work of Patrick Kavanagh.

Page 26: 'Invitation to My Sister' was inspired by Elizabeth Bishop's 'Invitation to Miss Marianne Moore' from her collection *Poems*.

Page 30: In 2006, when a digger was cutting turf, a book of psalms was unearthed from the Fadden More bog in County Tipperary, Ireland. Hidden for hundreds of years, the psalter is now on display in the National Museum of Ireland.

Page 33: 'When the Light' is in response to a painting by Naoko Sekine in Kisarazu City, Japan as part of the Telephone Project which was a global artistic collaboration online during the pandemic.

Page 35: Leaven, responding to a photograph as part of the Shorelines Festival 2020/1.

Page 41: 'For too long we have stretched the bowstring of air' the epigraph chosen for 'Taking Itself Back' is from the poem 'The Wind in Winter' from *Selected Poems* by Miroslav Holub (Penguin Modern European Poets, 1969).

The Other Side of Longing is a collaboration with US poet Lisa C. Taylor, and was chosen as the Elizabeth Gerson Lecture at the University of Connecticut for 2011.

Bone Road is a poetry memoir which charts the course of leavetaking and homecoming of my great grandparents and their six children, one of them my grandmother, who left Ireland in 1883 as part of the Tuke Assisted Emigration Scheme. They couldn't settle in America and returned to Ireland in November 1884.

About the Author

Geraldine Mills is a poet and fiction writer from County Galway. Her poetry collections are *Unearthing Your Own* (Bradshaw Books, 2001); *Toil the Dark Harvest* (Bradshaw Books, 2005); *An Urgency of Stars* (Arlen House, 2010); *The Other Side of Longing* (Arlen House, 2011); *Bone Road* (Arlen House, 2019); *Bone Road in Word and Image* (Arlen House, 2020). Her three short story collections, *Lick of the Lizard* (2005); *The Weight of Feathers* (2007) and *Hellkite* (2014) are also published by Arlen House. Her first children's novel, *Gold*, was published by Little Island in 2016, and its sequel, *Orchard*, was published by Andrena Press in 2021.

A winner of the Hennessy/*Sunday Tribune* New Irish Writer Award, she has been awarded three Arts Council Literature Bursaries, an Arts Council Covid 19 Crisis Award, and an Arts Council Agility Award. She is also a recipient of a Katherine Kavanagh Fellowship.

She collaborated with New England poet, Lisa C. Taylor, on the joint collection *The Other Side of Longing* (Arlen House) which was chosen as the Gerson Reading at the University of Connecticut in 2011. Her fiction and poetry have been on the curricula of contemporary literature courses at the University of Missouri, St Louis; Emory University, Georgia; University of Connecticut; Eastern Connecticut State University and Emerson College, MA, USA summer programme at the Burren College of Art. Her short story 'Pretty Bird, why you so sad?' has been featured on the state exams in Denmark.

When the Light: New and Selected Poems is her seventh poetry collection.

www.geraldinemills.com